many colors of mother goose

adapted by Cheryl Willis Hudson

illustrated by

Ken Brown, Mark Corcoran and Cathy Johnson

Just Us Books

East Orange, New Jersey

Many Colors of Mother Goose, copyright 1997 by Just Us Books, Inc.
Text adaptation copyright 1997 by Cheryl Willis Hudson.
Individual illustrations, copyright 1997 by Ken Brown, Mark Corcoran and Cathy Johnson.
All rights reserved. No part of this book may be reproduced or utilized in any form or
by any means, electronic or mechanical, including photocopying, recording or by any information storage
and retrieval system without permission in writing from the publisher. Inquiries should be addressed to
JUST US BOOKS, INC. 356 Glenwood Ave., East Orange, NJ 07017

Printed in China/First Edition 10 9 8 7 6 5 4
Library of Congress Catalog Number 97-7397
ISBN: 0-940975-91-2

Cataloging in publication data is available.

JUST US BOOKS
East Orange, NJ

contents

there was an old woman

There was an old woman
Who lived in a shoe.
She cared for lots of children
And knew just what to do.

She gave them hugs and kisses—
She shared happy dreams and good wishes.
And they lived, laughed and loved
All year through.

early to bed

Rooster crows in the morning time
To tell all the children to rise.
For those who sleep late
Will never be wise.
Go to bed early.
Shut those droopy eyes.
For early to bed and early to rise
Makes children healthy and wealthy and wise.

hickory, dickory, dock

Hickory, Dickory, Dock!
Two mice ran up the clock.
The clock struck one.
The other was stunned.
Hickory, Dickory, Dock!

this little piggy

This little piggy went shopping.
This little piggy stayed home.
This little piggy had corn on the cob.
This little piggy had none.
And this little piggy cried,
"Oui, Oui, Oui!"
All the way home!

three blind mice

Three blind mice
See how they run.
They all ran after the farmer's wife.
She chased them back home,
With all of her might.
Did you ever see such a sight in your life?
As three blind mice.

three little kittens

Three little kittens, they lost their mittens
And they began to cry,
"Oh, Mommy dear, we greatly fear,
That we have lost our mittens".

"What! Lost your mittens?
You naughty kittens!
Then you shall have no pie.
Mee-ow, mee-ow, mee-ow,
Then you shall have no pie".

there was a
zig-zag man

There was a zig-zag man,
He walked a zig-zag mile,
He found a zig-zag walking stick
And had a zig-zag smile.
He bought a zig-zag cat,
Which caught a zig-zag mouse,
And they all lived together
In a little zig-zag house.

one, two, buckle my shoe

One, two,
Buckle my shoe.

Three, four,
Shut the door.

Five, six,
Pick up sticks.

Seven, eight,
Lay them straight.

Nine, ten,
A big fat hen.

Eleven, twelve,
Froggies in the well.

Thirteen, fourteen
Maids are courting.

Fifteen, sixteen,
Cooks in the kitchen.

Seventeen, eighteen,
School bus is waiting.

Nineteen, twenty,
The seats are all empty!

jack and jill

Jack and Jill
Went up the hill
To fetch a pail of water.
Jack fell down
And started to frown
Then Jill came tumbling after.

little ms. muffet
(or a few words to a. spider)

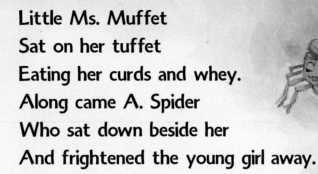

Little Ms. Muffet
Sat on her tuffet
Eating her curds and whey.
Along came A. Spider
Who sat down beside her
And frightened the young girl away.

But Little Ms. Muffet
Decided to tough it.
She glarred at the spider who'd scared her.
Shouted she to Anansi,
"No spider can bully me!"
"Give me credit for courage, kind sir!"

"I know you're a trickster.
And I'll be in a fix, sir
If you spoil my first meal of the day.
Breakfast is key!
I won't let you scare me.
I'll finish my meal, anyway!"

little boy lou

Little Boy Lou,
Come blow your horn.
We're jammin' in New Orleans
Where jazz bands are born.
Let's go find musicians
Who can keep the beat.
The parade is starting right now
Down on Bourbon Street.

georgie, porgie, puddin' and pie

Georgie, Porgie, Puddin' and Pie
Were kids who sang
In the talent show
At Eastside Junior High.

little bo peep

Little Bo Peep
Lost her sheep
And didn't know where to find them.

They played hide and seek
Near the woods and the creek
While wagging their tails behind them.

peter, peter, pumpkin eater

Peter, Peter, pumpkin eater
Had a wife, was pleased to greet her.
He built a house like a pumpkin shell
And there they both lived very well.

Nina, Nina, was her name.
She loved her husband just the same.
Often she baked him sweet potato pie
Which made him an even more pleasant guy.

zack sprat

Zack Sprat refused meat and fat.
His wife, Pam, refused to eat lean.
And so the both of them were known
As a fruit and vegetable team.

rub a dub dub

Rub A Dub Dub
Three kids in a tub.
Who could they possibly be?
A dancer, a painter,
And a video-maker
Adrift on a make believe sea.

ring around the rosies

Ring around the rosies.
Wiggle all your toes-ies.
Jump up, dance around,
We all fall down!

i'm glad the sky is painted blue

I'm glad the sky is painted blue
And earth is painted green.
With a rainbow of colors for boys and girls
All sandwiched in between.

magic words

s'il vous plait
por favor
per favore
b'vak hashan
please

There are two little magic words
That will open any door with ease.
One little word is "Thanks".
And the other little word is "Please".

merci beaucoup
gracia
grazie
to dah
thanks

rain, rain, go away

Rain, rain, go away.
Come again some other day.
Little Donna wants to play.
So rain, rain, go away.

Pat a cake **pat a cake**
Pat a cake
Baker's man
Make me a cake
As fast as you can.
Roll it and pat it
And mark it with a ß
And put it in the oven
For Baby and me!

hush little baby,
don't say a word

Hush, little baby, don't say a word.

Papa's going to buy you a mocking bird.

If that mocking bird won't sing,

Papa's going to buy you a diamond ring.

If that diamond ring turns to brass,

Papa's going to buy you a looking glass.

If that looking glass gets broke,

Papa's going to buy you a billy goat.

If that billy goat starts to bite,

Papa's going to buy you a cart and kite.

And if that cart and kite fall down

You'll still be the prettiest baby in town.

sing a song of six gents

Sing a song of six gents
Waiting in the deli.
One corned beef on rye,
for Kent.
A veggie burger for Kelly.

Ham and cheese for Vito.
With pickles on the side.
Pizza pie for Harry.
And tuna fish for Clyde.

Slice the sub for Manuel
Cheese and fries are extra.
Take a ticket, start again.
This deli's great, you bet'cha.

Ole King Cole was a partying old soul
And a partying old soul was he.
To get things started on the dance floor,
He called for his fiddlers three.

They played blue grass and soul,
Hip hop and rock 'n roll.
They also played the waltz and minuette.
No matter the crowd's taste in music,
King Cole shouted royally,
"Just choose it!
My cats are the best you can get!"

the queen of hearts

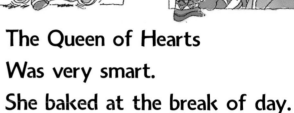

The Queen of Hearts
Was very smart.
She baked at the break of day.

The Knave of Hearts
Stole a shopping cart
And carried her baked goods away.

The King of Hearts
Called for the tarts
And punished the Knave full sore.

The Knave of Hearts
Brought back the tarts
And vowed he would steal
no more.

heavy deebert

Heavy Deebert sat on a wall.
He made up funny rhymes
With sound effects and all.
All of his neighbors and all of his friends
Were happy to have him do it again.

hey, diddle, diddle!

Hey, diddle, diddle,

The cat played the fiddle,

And the cow danced a jig to his tune.

The little dog giggled.

Beneath the stars and moon.

And the dish pranced in space with the spoon.

a wise old owl

A wise old owl sat in an oak.

The more she heard the less she spoke.

The less she spoke the more she heard.

Why aren't we all like that wise old bird?

twinkle, twinkle, little star

Twinkle, twinkle little star,
I wonder how far away you are.
Up above the world so high
Like a diamond in the sky.

star light, star bright

Star light, star bright,
First star I see tonight.
I wish I may,
I wish I might
Have the wish
I wish tonight!

i see the moon

I see the moon
And the moon sees me.
God bless the moon.
God bless me.

About many colors of mother goose

Traditional rhymes of Mother Goose have been revitalized and updated in this illustrated collection. Through verse and art, this "new" Mother Goose reflects the flavor of American's cultural and ethnic diversity. A number of the rhymes have been given a contemporary feel.

"Little Boy Blue", for instance, is rendered as "Little Boy Lou", a young boy who plays his horn on a neighborhood street. Could "Little Boy Lou" embody the spirit of the great jazz musician, Louis Armstrong? "Sing a Song of Six Pence" has become "Sing a Song of Six Gents", and the six gents are a colorful group who work in a delicatessen. "Ole King Cole" is still merry, but he now enjoys different kinds of music such as jazz and rock.

While *MANY COLORS OF MOTHER GOOSE* reflects both traditional and contemporary childhood themes and celebrates diversity, it is also sheer fun. This collection possesses the same magic that has enthralled children and adults throughout the years.

Cheryl Willis Hudson is a graphic designer and the editor of *MANY COLORS OF MOTHER GOOSE*. She is the author of *AFRO-BETS ABC BOOK*; co-author with Bernette G. Ford of *BRIGHT EYES, BROWN SKIN*; and compiler with her husband Wade Hudson, of *IN PRAISE OF OUR FATHERS AND OUR MOTHERS, A BLACK FAMILY TREASURY BY OUTSTANDING AUTHORS AND ARTISTS*. A native of Portsmouth, Virginia, she now lives with her family in New Jersey.

Ken Brown is a veteran illustrator of the advertising and publishing industry. A native of Philadelphia, he studied illustration and advertising at Art Center of Design in California. His clients include Essence Magazine, Proctor and Gamble, Pennsylvania Board of Education and Huggy Bean. Ken's illustrations appear on pages 1, 4, 5, 14, 15, 17, 26, 27, 30, 31 and on the back cover.

Mark Corcoran loves to illustrate animals and humorous situations. From his studio in New York City he works on illustrations that appear in many school reading books found in classrooms across the United States. His illustrations appear on pages 3, 6, 7, 8, 9, 16, 24, 25, 28, 29 and on the back cover.

Cathy Johnson studied art at Columbus College of Art and Design in Columbus, Ohio. She and her son live in Kansas City, Missouri, where she designs products for children including toys, greeting cards and posters. *MANY COLORS OF MOTHER GOOSE* is her first trade picture book. Her illustrations appear on pages 10, 11, 12, 13, 18, 19, 20, 21, 22, 23 and on the front cover.

Cover and text design by Carol T. Jenkins, Jenkins Graphics, East Orange, NJ